Your Cooking Guide

Clean Eating Cuisine

Tasty and Nutrient-Dense Recipes for Healthy Living

BY Terra Compasso

Licensing and Copyrighting

Table of Contents

Introduction

This comprehensive resource is designed to simplify your journey towards a healthier, more nourishing lifestyle. Whether you're a beginner or well-versed in clean eating, this guide offers valuable insights and practical tips to make your transition seamless and enjoyable. Clean eating is all about embracing whole, unprocessed foods that provide optimal nutrition and support your overall well-being. In this guide, we break down the principles of clean eating into easy-to-understand concepts, helping you understand the benefits and science behind it. You'll discover a wealth of information on how to incorporate fresh fruits, vegetables, lean proteins, and whole grains into your daily meals. We provide guidance on meal planning, grocery shopping, and mindful eating, empowering you to make informed choices that nourish your body.

Whether you're looking to boost your energy levels, achieve your ideal weight, or simply improve your overall health, This book is your go-to resource. Get ready to embark on a transformative journey towards vibrant health and wellness. Let's begin!

xxxxxxxxxxxxxxxxxxxxxxxxxxxxxxxxxx

1. Chicken Veggie Packets

Chicken Veggie Packets are a delightful and convenient meal option. Succulent chicken breast, along with a colorful assortment of fresh vegetables, is seasoned, wrapped in foil, and baked to perfection. This dish is not only delicious but also healthy, making it a perfect choice for busy individuals seeking a nutritious and flavorful meal.

Preparation Time: 10 minutes

Cook time: 20 minutes

Total: 30 minutes

Serves: 4

Ingredients:

Kitchen Tools Needed:

- Aluminum foil
- Baking sheet
- 4 chicken breasts
- 2 cups of mixed vegetables
- 4 tablespoons of olive oil
- Salt and pepper to taste.

xxxxxxxxxxxxxxxxxxxxxxxxxxxxxxxx

Instructions:

a. Set the oven to 375°F.

b. Cut 4 large pieces of aluminum foil.

c. Place a chicken breast on each piece of foil.

d. Divide the mixed vegetables evenly among the chicken breasts.

e. Drizzle each chicken and vegetable packet with 1 tablespoon of olive oil.

f. Season with salt and pepper to taste.

g. Fold the foil over the chicken and vegetables to create a packet.

h. Place the packets on a baking sheet.

i. Bake for 35 minutes or until the chicken is cooked through and the vegetables are tender.

2. Calico Scrambled Eggs

Calico Scrambled Eggs are a vibrant and flavorful twist on traditional scrambled eggs. This delightful dish combines fluffy scrambled eggs with a colorful medley of diced bell peppers, onions, and tomatoes. The result is a visually appealing and delicious breakfast or brunch option that will leave your taste buds satisfied.

Preparation Time: 10 minutes

Cook time: 20 minutes

Total: 30 minutes

Serves: 4

Ingredients:

- 1/4 cup diced yellow bell pepper.
- 1/4 cup diced onion.
- 1/4 cup shredded cheddar chees
- Salt and pepper to taste.
- 4 large eggs
- 1/4 cup diced red bell pepper.
- 1/4 cup diced green bell pepper.
- 1/4 cup diced tomato.

xxxxxxxxxxxxxxxxxxxxxxxxxxxxxxxxxx

Instructions:

a. In a bowl, beat the eggs until well mixed.
b. Heat the frying pan over medium heat.
c. Add the diced bell peppers and onion to the pan and sauté until they start to soften.
d. Add the diced tomato to the pan and sauté for another minute.
e. Pour the beaten eggs into the pan and stir gently with a spatula.
f. Continue stirring the eggs until they are cooked to your desired consistency.
g. Sprinkle the shredded cheddar cheese over the cooked eggs and stir until melted.
h. Season with salt and pepper to taste.
i. Serve the Calico Scrambled Eggs hot.

3. Salmon with Tomato-Goat Cheese Couscous

Salmon with Tomato-Goat Cheese Couscous is a mouthwatering and nutritious meal. Grilled salmon fillets are served on a bed of fluffy couscous mixed with tangy tomato and creamy goat cheese. This flavorful combination creates a delightful balance of textures and flavors, making it a delightful choice for any seafood lover.

Preparation Time: 5 minutes

Cook time: 25 minutes

Total: 30 minutes

Serves: 4

Ingredients:

- Tomatoes
- Goat cheese
- Couscous
- Fresh basil
- Salt
- Pepper
- Salmon fillets
- Olive oil
- Garlic

xxxxxxxxxxxxxxxxxxxxxxxxxxxxxxxx

Instructions:

a. Set the oven to 400°F (200°C).

b. Arrange the salmon fillets on a baking pan lined with parchment paper.

c. Season the salmon with salt and pepper.

d. Bake the salmon in the preheated oven for 15-20 minutes, or until cooked through.

e. Meanwhile, cook the couscous according to package instructions.

f. In a frying pan, heat olive oil over medium heat.

g. Add minced garlic and sauté until fragrant.

h. Add diced tomatoes and cook until softened.

i. Stir in crumbled goat cheese until melted and well combined.

j. Remove from heat and stir in cooked couscous.

k. Season with salt and pepper to taste.

l. Serve the salmon over the tomato-goat cheese couscous.

m. Garnish with fresh basil leaves.

4. Loaded Quinoa Breakfast Bowl

The Loaded Quinoa Breakfast Bowl is a hearty and nutritious way to start your day. This bowl is packed with protein-rich quinoa, topped with a variety of delicious ingredients such as avocado, eggs, spinach, and cherry tomatoes. It's a wholesome and satisfying breakfast option that will keep you energized throughout the morning.

Preparation Time: 5 minutes

Cook time: 25 minutes

Total: 30 minutes

Serves: 1

Ingredients:

- 1/2 cup mixed berries
- 1 tablespoon honey
- 1 tablespoon shredded coconut
- 1 tablespoon sliced almonds
- 1/2 cup quinoa
- 1 cup almond milk
- 1 tablespoon chia seeds
- 1 tablespoon almond butter

xxxxxxxxxxxxxxxxxxxxxxxxxxxxxxxxx

Instructions:

a. Rinse the quinoa under cold water.
b. Combine the quinoa and almond milk in a medium pot.
c. Boiling at a medium heat setting. Once the quinoa is cooked and the liquid has been absorbed, reduce the heat to low and let it stew for 15 to 20 minutes.
d. Turn off the heat and let the food rest for 5 minutes.
e. Fluff the quinoa with a fork.
f. Transfer the quinoa to a serving bowl.
g. Top with mixed berries, honey, chia seeds, almond butter, shredded coconut, and sliced almonds.
h. Enjoy your Loaded Quinoa Breakfast Bowl!

5. Saucy Mediterranean Chicken with Rice

Saucy Mediterranean Chicken with Rice is a flavorful and satisfying dish that brings the vibrant flavors of the Mediterranean to your plate. Tender chicken is cooked in a delicious tomato-based sauce with herbs, spices, and olives, served over a bed of fluffy rice. It's a delicious and comforting meal that will transport you to the Mediterranean coast.

Preparation Time: 5 minutes

Cook time: 25 minutes

Total: 30 minutes

Serves: 4

Ingredients:

- 1 onion, diced.
- 1 red bell pepper, sliced.
- 1 yellow bell pepper, sliced.
- 1 can of diced tomatoes
- 1 teaspoon of dried oregano
- 1 teaspoon of dried basil
- Salt and pepper to taste.
- 4 chicken breasts
- 1 cup of rice
- 2 cloves of garlic, minced.
- 1/2 cup of black olives, sliced.
- 1 tablespoon of olive oil

XXXXXXXXXXXXXXXXXXXXXXXXXXXXXXXXX

Instructions:

a. Cook the rice according to package instructions.

b. Season the chicken breasts with salt, pepper, dried basil, and dried oregano.

c. In a large skillet, heat olive oil over medium heat.

d. Add the chicken breasts to the skillet then cook about 5-6 minutes per side, or till cooked through.

e. Remove the chicken from the skillet and set aside.

f. In the same skillet, add the minced garlic, diced onion, and sliced bell peppers.

g. Cook for 5 minutes, or until the vegetables are tender.

h. Add the can of diced tomatoes and black olives to the skillet.

i. Bring the mixture to a simmer and cook for 10 minutes.

j. Slice the cooked chicken breasts and add them back to the skillet.

k. Cook for an additional 5 minutes, or until everything is heated through.

l. Serve the saucy Mediterranean chicken over cooked rice.

m. Enjoy!

6. Sweet Potato and Egg Skillet

The Sweet Potato and Egg Skillet is a delicious and nutritious breakfast or brunch option. Sautéed sweet potatoes are combined with onions, peppers, and spices, creating a flavorful base. Topped with perfectly cooked eggs, it's a satisfying and wholesome dish that will fuel your day with a burst of flavors.

Preparation Time: 5 minutes

Cook time: 20 minutes

Total: 25 minutes

Serves: 4

Ingredients:

- 1 red bell pepper
- 1 green bell pepper
- 1 tablespoon olive oil
- Salt and pepper to taste.
- 2 sweet potatoes
- 4 eggs
- 1 onion
- 2 cloves of garlic

xxxxxxxxxxxxxxxxxxxxxxxxxxxxxxxxx

Instructions:

a. Peel and dice the sweet potatoes into small cubes.

b. Chop the onion, garlic, and bell peppers.

c. Heat the olive oil in a skillet over medium heat.

d. Add the diced sweet potatoes to the skillet and cook for about 10 minutes, or until they are slightly tender.

e. Add the chopped onion, garlic, and bell peppers to the skillet and cook for another 5 minutes.

f. In the sweet potato mixture, make four wells, and put an egg into each one.

g. Cover the skillet and cook for about 7-10 minutes, or until the eggs are cooked to your liking.

h. Season with salt and pepper to taste.

i. Serve the sweet potato and egg skillet hot.

7. Cod and Asparagus Bake

The Cod and Asparagus Bake is a delightful and healthy seafood dish. Tender cod fillets are paired with fresh asparagus spears, drizzled with lemon juice, and baked to perfection. This flavorful combination creates a light and delicious meal that showcases the natural flavors of the fish and vegetables.

Preparation Time: 5 minutes

Cook time: 40 minutes

Total: 45 minutes

Serves: 4

Ingredients:

- Olive oil
- Garlic
- Salt
- Pepper
- Cod fillets
- Asparagus
- Lemon

xxxxxxxxxxxxxxxxxxxxxxxxxxxxxxxx

Instructions:

a. Set the oven to 400°F (200°C).

b. Place the cod fillets in a baking dish and season with pepper and salt.

c. Trim the ends of the asparagus then arrange them around the cod fillets in the baking dish.

d. Drizzle olive oil over the cod and asparagus.

e. Squeeze lemon juice over the cod and asparagus.

f. Mince garlic and sprinkle it over the cod and asparagus.

g. Cover the baking dish with aluminum foil.

h. Bake in the preheated oven for 20 minutes.

i. Remove the foil and bake for an additional 10-15 minutes, or till the asparagus is tender and the cod is cooked through.

j. Serve hot and enjoy!

8. Smoky Cauliflower Bites

Smoky Cauliflower Bites are a tasty and nutritious snack or appetizer option. Roasted cauliflower florets are seasoned with smoky spices, creating a savory and satisfying flavor. These crispy bites are perfect for those looking for a healthy alternative to traditional finger foods, without sacrificing on taste.

Preparation Time: 5 minutes

Cook time: 25 minutes

Total: 30 minutes

Serves: 4

Ingredients:

- 1 teaspoon smoked paprika.
- 1/2 teaspoon garlic powder
- 1/4 teaspoon black pepper
- 1 head of cauliflower
- 2 tablespoons olive oil
- 1/2 teaspoon salt

xxxxxxxxxxxxxxxxxxxxxxxxxxxxxxxxx

Instructions:

a. Set the oven to 425°F (220°C).
b. Cut the cauliflower into bite-sized florets.
c. Whisk together smoked paprika, olive oil, garlic powder, black pepper, and salt in a mixing bowl.
d. Add the cauliflower florets to the bowl and toss until well coated.
e. On a baking sheet, spread the cauliflower florets in a single layer.
f. Bake in the preheated oven about 20-25 minutes, or till the cauliflower is slightly charred and tender.
g. Serve the smoky cauliflower bites hot as a delicious appetizer or side dish.

9. Grilled Chicken and Mango Skewers

Grilled Chicken and Mango Skewers are a delightful combination of savory and sweet flavors. Tender grilled chicken pieces are paired with juicy mango chunks, creating a mouthwatering contrast. These skewers make for a perfect summer dish, providing a burst of tropical goodness with every bite.

Preparation Time: 5 minutes

Cook time: 25 minutes

Total: 30 minutes

Serves: 4

Ingredients:

- 1 red onion
- 2 tablespoons olive oil
- 2 tablespoons lime juice
- 1/2 teaspoon cumin
- Salt and pepper to taste.
- 4 boneless, skinless chicken breasts
- 2 ripe mangoes
- 1 red bell pepper
- 1 teaspoon chili powder

xxxxxxxxxxxxxxxxxxxxxxxxxxxxxxxx

Instructions:

a. Set the grill to medium heat.

b. Cut the chicken breasts into bite-sized pieces.

c. Peel and dice the mangoes and chop the bell pepper and red onion into chunks.

d. In a bowl, whisk together the olive oil, lime juice, cumin, chili powder, salt, and pepper.

e. Thread the chicken, mangoes, bell pepper, and red onion onto skewers, alternating between ingredients.

f. Brush the skewers with the marinade mixture.

g. Place the skewers on the preheated grill and cook for about 10-12 minutes, turning occasionally, until the chicken is cooked through, and the mangoes are slightly caramelized.

h. Remove the skewers from the grill and let them rest for a few minutes before serving.

i. Serve the grilled chicken and mango skewers hot and enjoy!

10. Tandoori Spiced Chicken Pita Pizza with Greek Yogurt and Cilantro

Tandoori Spiced Chicken Pita Pizza with Greek Yogurt and Cilantro is a fusion of flavors that will tantalize your taste buds. Tender tandoori spiced chicken, fresh cilantro, and creamy Greek yogurt come together on a crispy pita bread crust. This unique and delicious pizza is a delightful twist on a classic favorite.

Preparation Time: 5 minutes

Cook time: 25 minutes

Total: 30 minutes

Serves: 4

Ingredients:

- 2 cups cooked chicken, shredded.
- 1/4 cup cilantro, chopped.
- 1/2 cup red onion thinly sliced.
- 1/2 cup cucumber, diced.
- 1/4 cup feta cheese, crumbled.
- 1 tablespoon olive oil
- Salt and pepper to taste.
- 4 whole wheat pita bread
- 1/2 cup Greek yogurt
- 1/2 cup cherry tomatoes, halved.
- 1 tablespoon tandoori spice mix

xxxxxxxxxxxxxxxxxxxxxxxxxxxxxxxx

Instructions:

a. Set the oven to 400°F (200°C).

b. In a mixing bowl, combine the shredded chicken, tandoori spice mix, olive oil, salt, and pepper. Mix well to coat the chicken with the spices.

c. Place the pita bread on a baking sheet and spread a thin layer of Greek yogurt on each pita.

d. Divide the spiced chicken evenly among the pitas, spreading it over the yogurt.

e. Top each pita with red onion, cherry tomatoes, cucumber, and feta cheese.

f. Bake in the preheated oven for 10-12 minutes, or until the pitas are crispy and the toppings are heated through.

g. Remove from the oven and garnish with chopped cilantro.

h. Slice the pita pizzas into quarters and serve hot.

11. Shrimp Avocado Salad

Shrimp Avocado Salad is a refreshing and nutritious dish that combines the flavors of succulent shrimp and creamy avocado. This vibrant salad is filled with fresh vegetables, herbs, and a tangy dressing, creating a light and satisfying meal that is perfect for warm weather or a quick and healthy lunch option.

Preparation Time: 5 minutes

Cook time: 25 minutes

Total: 30 minutes

Serves: 4

Ingredients:

- Avocado
- Lettuce
- Red onion
- Cilantro
- Lime juice
- Salt
- Black pepper
- Shrimp
- Cherry tomatoes
- Olive oil

xxxxxxxxxxxxxxxxxxxxxxxxxxxxxxxx

Instructions:

a. Peel and devein the shrimp.
b. In a medium bowl, combine the shrimp, diced avocado, lettuce, cherry tomatoes, thinly sliced red onion, and chopped cilantro.
c. In a small bowl, whisk together olive oil, salt, lime juice, and black pepper to make the dressing.
d. Pour the dressing over the salad and toss to combine.
e. Serve the shrimp avocado salad chilled.

12. Shrimp Scampi Spinach Salad

Shrimp Scampi Spinach Salad is a delightful combination of flavors and textures. Succulent shrimp, cooked in a garlic butter sauce, is tossed with fresh spinach leaves, cherry tomatoes, and a zesty lemon dressing. This salad offers a perfect balance of lightness and richness, making it a delicious and satisfying meal option.

Preparation Time: 5 minutes

Cook time: 25 minutes

Total: 30 minutes

Serves: 4

Ingredients:

- Garlic
- Butter
- Lemon Juice
- Spinach
- Cherry Tomatoes
- Parmesan Cheese
- Salt
- Black Pepper
- Shrimp
- White Wine
- Red Onion

xxxxxxxxxxxxxxxxxxxxxxxxxxxxxxxx

Instructions:

a. In a skillet, melt the butter over medium heat.

b. Add the garlic and cook until fragrant.

c. Add the shrimp and cook until pink.

d. Remove the shrimp from the skillet and set aside.

e. In a mixing bowl, whisk together the lemon juice, white wine, salt, and black pepper.

f. Add the spinach, cherry tomatoes, and red onion to the mixing bowl.

g. Toss the salad ingredients until well coated.

h. Divide the salad onto 4 plates.

i. Top each plate with the cooked shrimp.

j. Sprinkle Parmesan cheese over the salad.

k. Serve and enjoy!

13. Garlic Chicken with Herbs

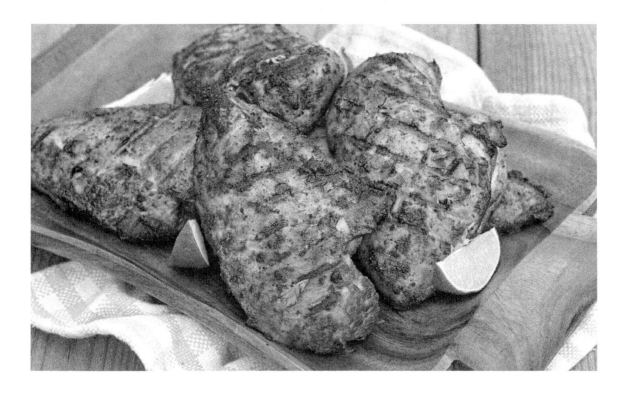

Garlic Chicken with Herbs is a flavorful and aromatic dish that will satisfy your taste buds. Succulent chicken breasts are marinated with garlic, herbs, and spices, creating a mouthwatering combination. This dish is perfect for any occasion, as it delivers a burst of savory flavors with every bite.

Preparation Time: 5 minutes

Cook time: 55 minutes

Total: 50 minutes

Serves: 4

Ingredients:

- 4 chicken breasts
- 1 tablespoon of mixed herbs
- salt and pepper to taste.
- 4 cloves of garlic

xxxxxxxxxxxxxxxxxxxxxxxxxxxxxxxx

Instructions:

a. Set the oven to 375°F (190°C).
b. Place the chicken breasts in a baking dish.
c. Peel and mince the garlic cloves.
d. Sprinkle the minced garlic, mixed herbs, salt, and pepper over the chicken breasts.
e. Cover the baking dish with foil then bake about 30 minutes.
f. Remove the foil before baking about an additional 15 minutes or till the chicken is cooked through.
g. Serve hot with your choice of side dishes.

14. Lemon–Parsley Tilapia

Lemon-Parsley Tilapia is a light and zesty seafood dish bursting with fresh flavors. Tender tilapia fillets are coated in a tangy lemon and parsley marinade, then pan-seared to perfection. This simple yet delicious recipe is a quick and healthy option for those seeking a flavorful and nutritious meal.

Preparation Time: 5 minutes

Cook time: 25 minutes

Total: 30 minutes

Serves: 4

Ingredients:

- Salt
- Pepper
- Olive oil
- Tilapia fillets
- Lemon
- Parsley

XXXXXXXXXXXXXXXXXXXXXXXXXXXXXXXX

Instructions:

a. Set the oven to 375°F.

b. In a mixing bowl, combine the chopped parsley, lemon zest, salt, and pepper.

c. In a baking dish, place the tilapia fillets and drizzle with olive oil.

d. Sprinkle the parsley mixture over the tilapia fillets.

e. Squeeze fresh lemon juice over the fillets.

f. Bake in the set the oven for 20-25 minutes, or till the fish is cooked through and flakes easily with a fork.

g. Serve hot and enjoy!

15. Veggie Steak Salad

Veggie Steak Salad is a delightful and satisfying meal that combines the heartiness of steak with the freshness of vegetables. Grilled or pan-seared steak slices are served on a bed of crisp lettuce, accompanied by an assortment of colorful veggies, creating a nutritious and flavorful salad that will leave you satisfied.

Preparation Time: 5 minutes

Cook time: 25 minutes

Total: 30 minutes

Serves: 4

Ingredients:

- Mixed salad greens
- Cherry tomatoes
- Red onion
- Bell pepper
- Olive oil
- Salt
- Black pepper
- Veggie steak
- Cucumber
- Balsamic vinegar

XXXXXXXXXXXXXXXXXXXXXXXXXXXXXXXXXX

Instructions:

a. Preheat the grill pan over medium heat.

b. Season the veggie steak with salt and black pepper.

c. Grill the veggie steak for about 5-7 minutes on each side, or until desired doneness.

d. Remove the veggie steak from the grill pan and let it rest for a few minutes.

e. Meanwhile, prepare the salad by combining the mixed salad greens, cherry tomatoes, sliced red onion, sliced cucumber, and diced bell pepper in a salad bowl.

f. In a separate small bowl, whisk together olive oil, balsamic vinegar, salt, and black pepper to make the dressing.

g. Slice the rested veggie steak into thin strips.

h. Add the sliced veggie steak to the salad bowl.

i. Drizzle the dressing over the salad and toss to combine.

j. Serve the veggie steak salad immediately and enjoy!

16. Grilled Jerk Shrimp Orzo Salad

Grilled Jerk Shrimp Orzo Salad is a vibrant and flavorful dish that combines the heat of jerk seasoning with succulent grilled shrimp. Served over a bed of orzo pasta and mixed with fresh vegetables and herbs, this salad is a refreshing and satisfying choice for a summer meal.

Preparation Time: 5 minutes

Cook time: 25 minutes

Total: 30 minutes

Serves: 2

Ingredients:

- Jerk seasoning
- Lime juice
- Red bell pepper
- Red onion
- Cilantro
- Shrimp
- Orzo
- Olive oil

xxxxxxxxxxxxxxxxxxxxxxxxxxxxxxxx

Instructions:

a. Preheat the grill.
b. Cook the orzo according to package instructions.
c. In a bowl, combine the shrimp, jerk seasoning, lime juice, and olive oil. Let marinate for 10 minutes.
d. Grill the shrimp until cooked through, about 2-3 minutes per side.
e. In a large bowl, combine the cooked orzo, grilled shrimp, red bell pepper, red onion, and cilantro.
f. Toss everything together until well combined.
g. Serve the grilled jerk shrimp orzo salad immediately.
h. Enjoy!

17. Kale Salad

Kale Salad is a nutritious and delicious choice for health-conscious individuals. This leafy green is packed with vitamins and minerals. Tossed with a tangy dressing, accompanied by crunchy toppings like nuts or seeds, it offers a satisfying combination of flavors and textures for a refreshing and wholesome salad experience.

Preparation Time: 5 minutes

Cook time: 25 minutes

Total: 30 minutes

Serves: 8

Ingredients:

- Lemon juice
- Salt
- Pepper
- Kale
- Olive oil

XXXXXXXXXXXXXXXXXXXXXXXXXXXXXXXXXX

Instructions:

a. Wash and dry the kale leaves.

b. Remove the tough stems and chop the leaves into bite-sized pieces.

c. In a bowl, whisk together olive oil, lemon juice, salt, and pepper to make the dressing.

d. Add the chopped kale to the bowl and toss well to coat it with the dressing.

e. Let the salad sit for about 10 minutes to allow the flavors to meld together.

f. Serve the kale salad as a side dish or add your favorite toppings like cherry tomatoes, avocado, or nuts for a complete meal.

18. Peppered Tuna Kabobs

Peppered Tuna Kabobs are a delectable and protein-packed dish. Fresh tuna steaks are coated with a flavorful blend of spices, then skewered and grilled to perfection. These kabobs offer a delightful combination of bold peppered flavors and succulent tuna, making them a delicious option for seafood lovers.

Preparation Time: 5 minutes

Cook time: 25 minutes

Total: 30 minutes

Serves: 4

Ingredients:

- Salt
- Olive oil
- Bell peppers
- Red onion
- Tuna steaks
- Black pepper
- Lemon juice

xxxxxxxxxxxxxxxxxxxxxxxxxxxxxxxxx

Instructions:

a. Preheat the grill to medium heat.

b. Cut the tuna steaks into bite-sized cubes.

c. In a small bowl, mix black pepper, salt, olive oil, and lemon juice to make a marinade.

d. Place the tuna cubes in the marinade and let them sit for 10 minutes.

e. Meanwhile, cut the bell peppers and red onion into bite-sized pieces.

f. Thread the marinated tuna cubes, bell peppers, and red onion onto skewers.

g. Brush the grill with olive oil to prevent sticking.

h. Grill the tuna kabobs for about 5 minutes on each side, or until the tuna is cooked to your liking.

i. Serve the peppered tuna kabobs hot with a side of salad or rice.

19. Full Garden Frittata

The Full Garden Frittata is a delightful and versatile dish filled with an array of fresh vegetables. This savory egg-based creation is loaded with vibrant flavors and textures, making it a perfect option for a satisfying breakfast, brunch, or light dinner. It's a wholesome and delicious way to enjoy a variety of garden-fresh ingredients.

Preparation Time: 5 minutes

Cook time: 25 minutes

Total: 30 minutes

Serves: 2

Ingredients:

- 1/4 cup milk
- 1/4 teaspoon black pepper
- 2 tablespoons olive oil
- 1/2 cup diced onion.
- 1/2 cup diced zucchini.
- 1/4 cup shredded cheddar cheese
- 1/4 cup chopped fresh parsley.
- 6 large eggs
- 1/2 teaspoon salt
- 1/2 cup diced bell pepper.
- 1/2 cup diced tomato.

xxxxxxxxxxxxxxxxxxxxxxxxxxxxxxx

Instructions:

a. In a mixing bowl, whisk together the eggs, milk, black pepper, and salt.

b. Heat olive oil in a non-stick skillet over medium heat.

c. Add the onion, bell pepper, zucchini, and tomato to the skillet. Sauté for 5 minutes or till the vegetables are tender.

d. In the skillet, pour the egg mixture over the sautéed vegetables.

e. Cook for 10-12 minutes or until the edges are set and the center is slightly jiggly.

f. Sprinkle shredded cheddar cheese and chopped fresh parsley over the top of the frittata.

g. Cover the skillet and cook for an additional 2-3 minutes or till the center is set and the cheese is melted.

h. Remove from heat and let it cool about 2-3 minutes before serving.

20. Grilled Basil Chicken

Grilled Basil Chicken is a mouthwatering dish bursting with fragrant flavors. Succulent chicken breasts are marinated in a delightful blend of basil, garlic, and spices, then grilled to perfection. This dish offers a perfect balance of herbs and charred smokiness, making it a delightful choice for any occasion.

Preparation Time: 5 minutes

Cook time: 25 minutes

Total: 30 minutes

Serves: 4

Ingredients:

- 1/4 cup fresh basil leaves
- 2 tablespoons olive oil
- Salt and pepper to taste.
- 4 chicken breasts
- 2 cloves garlic

xxxxxxxxxxxxxxxxxxxxxxxxxxxxxxxxx

Instructions:

a. Preheat the grill to medium heat.

b. In a food processor, combine the basil leaves, garlic, olive oil, salt, and pepper. Process until well combined.

c. Rub the basil mixture onto both sides of the chicken breasts.

d. On the preheated grill, place the chicken breasts then cook around 6-8 minutes on each side, or till the internal temperature reaches 165°F.

e. Remove the chicken from the grill and let it rest for a few minutes before serving.

f. Serve the grilled basil chicken with your favorite side dishes.

g. Enjoy!

21. Mediterranean Broccoli & Cheese Omelet

The Mediterranean Broccoli & Cheese Omelet is a savory and nutritious breakfast option. Loaded with vibrant flavors, this omelet combines fluffy eggs, tender broccoli florets, tangy feta cheese, and Mediterranean herbs. It's a delightful way to start your day with a burst of Mediterranean-inspired goodness in every bite.

Preparation Time: 5 minutes

Cook time: 25 minutes

Total: 30 minutes

Serves: 4

Ingredients:

- 1/4 cup black olives, sliced.
- 1/4 cup sun-dried tomatoes, chopped.
- 2 tablespoons olive oil
- Salt and pepper to taste.
- 6 large eggs
- 1 cup broccoli florets
- 1/2 cup feta cheese, crumbled.

xxxxxxxxxxxxxxxxxxxxxxxxxxxxxxxxx

Instructions:

a. In a bowl, whisk the eggs until well beaten.

b. In a nonstick frying pan, heat the olive oil over medium heat.

c. Add broccoli florets and cook for 5 minutes until slightly tender.

d. Pour the beaten eggs into the pan, spreading evenly.

e. Cook for 2-3 minutes until the edges start to set.

f. Sprinkle feta cheese, black olives, and sun-dried tomatoes over half of the omelet.

g. Fold the other half of the omelet over the filling.

h. Cook for another 2-3 minutes until the cheese melts and the omelet is cooked through.

i. Season with salt and pepper to taste.

j. Remove from heat and serve hot.

22. Roasted Pumpkin and Brussels Sprouts

Roasted Pumpkin and Brussels Sprouts is a delightful autumn dish. The combination of tender roasted pumpkin cubes and crispy Brussels sprouts creates a perfect balance of flavors and textures. This hearty and flavorful side dish is a wonderful addition to any meal, adding a touch of seasonal goodness to your plate.

Preparation Time: 10 minutes

Cook time: 45 minutes

Total: 55 minutes

Serves: 8

Ingredients:

- Olive Oil
- Salt
- Black Pepper
- Pumpkin
- Brussels Sprouts

xxxxxxxxxxxxxxxxxxxxxxxxxxxxxxxxx

Instructions:

a. Set the oven to 400°F (200°C).

b. Chop the sprouts from the Brussels and cube the pumpkin.

c. On a baking sheet, place the sprouts from Brussels and pumpkin cubes.

d. Add pepper and salt and drizzle with olive oil.

e. Roast in the oven for 40-45 minutes, or till the vegetables are tender and slightly caramelized.

f. Serve hot and enjoy!

23. Sheet-Pan Chicken and Vegetables

Sheet-Pan Chicken and Vegetables is a convenient and wholesome meal. Succulent chicken pieces, along with an assortment of colorful vegetables, are seasoned and roasted on a single sheet pan. This simple yet flavorful dish offers a well-rounded combination of protein and nutrients, making it a go-to option for busy weeknight dinners.

Preparation Time: 15 minutes

Cook time: 45 minutes

Total: 1 hour

Serves: 6

Ingredients:

- 1 pound baby carrots
- 1 red bell pepper, sliced.
- 1 yellow bell pepper, sliced.
- 4 cloves garlic, minced.
- 2 tablespoons olive oil
- 1 teaspoon paprika
- Salt and pepper to taste.
- 6 boneless, skinless chicken breasts
- 1 pound baby potatoes, halved.
- 1 red onion, sliced.
- 1 teaspoon dried thyme
- 1 teaspoon dried rosemary

xxxxxxxxxxxxxxxxxxxxxxxxxxxxxxxx

Instructions:

a. Set the oven to 425°F (220°C).

b. In a mixing bowl, combine the olive oil, dried thyme, minced garlic, dried rosemary, paprika, salt, and pepper.

c. Place the chicken breasts on the sheet pan and brush them with the olive oil mixture.

d. Arrange the baby potatoes, baby carrots, bell peppers, and red onion around the chicken on the sheet pan.

e. Drizzle the remaining olive oil mixture over the vegetables.

f. Season the vegetables with salt and pepper.

g. Bake for 40-45 minutes on a sheet pan in a preheated oven, or until the chicken has been cooked through and the vegetables are tender.

h. Removed from the oven and set aside for a few minutes before serving.

i. Serve the Sheet-Pan Chicken and Vegetables hot and enjoy!

24. Chicken Veggie Skillet

The Chicken Veggie Skillet is a delicious and nutritious one-pan meal. Tender chicken pieces are cooked alongside a medley of fresh vegetables, creating a flavorful and wholesome dish. With its convenience and variety of flavors, this skillet is a perfect choice for a quick and satisfying dinner option.

Preparation Time: 15 minutes

Cook time: 30 minutes

Total: 45 minutes

Serves: 6

Ingredients:

- Assorted vegetables (e.g., bell peppers, zucchini, carrots)
- Olive oil
- Salt
- Onion powder
- Paprika
- Dried herbs (e.g., thyme, rosemary, oregano)
- Chicken breast
- Pepper
- Garlic powder

xxxxxxxxxxxxxxxxxxxxxxxxxxxxxxxx

Instructions:

a. Cut the chicken breast into bite-sized pieces.
b. Heat olive oil in a skillet or frying pan over medium heat.
c. Add the chicken pieces to the skillet and cook until browned on all sides.
d. Remove the chicken from the skillet and set aside.
e. In the same skillet, add the assorted vegetables and cook until they start to soften.
f. Season the vegetables with salt, pepper, garlic powder, onion powder, paprika, and dried herbs.
g. Return the cooked chicken to the skillet and stir to combine with the vegetables.
h. Cook for another 5-10 minutes, or until the chicken is cooked through and the vegetables are tender.
i. Serve hot and enjoy!

25. Pizzaiola Chops

Pizzaiola Chops are a mouthwatering and savory dish. Thick, juicy pork chops are smothered in a rich tomato sauce infused with garlic, oregano, and other Italian herbs. This flavorful and comforting meal is reminiscent of a classic pizzaiola, bringing a taste of Italy to your plate.

Preparation Time: 15 minutes

Cook time: 30 minutes

Total: 45 minutes

Serves: 4

Ingredients:

- 1 onion, sliced.
- 1 can (14 ounces) diced tomatoes.
- 1/2 teaspoon dried oregano
- Salt and pepper to taste.
- 1/4 cup grated Parmesan cheese.
- 4 pork chops
- 1 tablespoon olive oil
- 2 cloves garlic, minced.
- 1/2 teaspoon dried basil

xxxxxxxxxxxxxxxxxxxxxxxxxxxxxxxxxx

Instructions:

a. Heat olive oil in a skillet over medium heat.

b. Add the pork chops and cook for 4-5 minutes per side, until browned.

c. Remove the pork chops from the skillet and set aside.

d. In the same skillet, add the sliced onion and minced garlic. Cook until the onion is softened.

e. Add the diced tomatoes, dried basil, dried oregano, salt, and pepper to the skillet. Stir to combine.

f. Return the pork chops to the skillet and spoon the tomato mixture over them. Cover the skillet and simmer for 15-20 minutes, until the pork chops are cooked through.

g. Sprinkle grated Parmesan cheese over the pork chops before serving.

26. Garlic Tilapia with Spicy Kale

Garlic Tilapia with Spicy Kale is a delightful and well-balanced meal. Tender tilapia fillets are seasoned with garlic and pan-seared to perfection, while the spicy kale adds a kick of flavor and nutrients. This dish offers a harmonious combination of flavors that will satisfy your taste buds and nourish your body.

Preparation Time: 15 minutes

Cook time: 20 minutes

Total: 35 minutes

Serves: 4

Ingredients:

- 1 teaspoon paprika
- 1/2 teaspoon salt
- 1/4 teaspoon black pepper
- 1 bunch of kale, stems removed, and leaves chopped.
- 1 tablespoon soy sauce
- 4 tilapia fillets
- 4 cloves of garlic, minced.
- 2 tablespoons olive oil
- 1 tablespoon red pepper flakes

xxxxxxxxxxxxxxxxxxxxxxxxxxxxxxxxx

Instructions:

a. Set the oven to 400°F (200°C).

b. In a mixing bowl, combine the minced garlic, olive oil, paprika, salt, and black pepper.

c. Place the tilapia fillets on a baking sheet and brush the garlic mixture over each fillet.

d. Bake the tilapia in the preheated oven for 15-20 minutes, or until cooked through.

e. While the tilapia is baking, heat a large skillet over medium heat.

f. Add the chopped kale to the skillet and sauté for 5 minutes, or until wilted.

g. Sprinkle the red pepper flakes and soy sauce over the kale and continue to cook for an additional 2 minutes.

h. Serve the garlic tilapia over a bed of spicy kale.

i. Enjoy!

27. Basil Vegetable Strata

Basil Vegetable Strata is a flavorful and satisfying dish that combines the goodness of fresh vegetables and aromatic basil. Layers of vegetables, bread, and cheese are baked to perfection, creating a savory and comforting casserole. This dish is perfect for brunch or a hearty vegetarian meal.

Preparation Time: 40 minutes

Cook time: 1 hour

Total: 1 hour 40 minutes

Serves: 8

Ingredients:

- Bread
- Cheese
- Salt
- Pepper
- Basil leaves
- Vegetables
- Eggs
- Milk

XXXXXXXXXXXXXXXXXXXXXXXXXXXXXXXXXX

Instructions:

a. Set the oven to 350°F (175°C).

b. Grease a baking dish with butter or cooking spray.

c. Slice the bread into thick slices and arrange them in the greased baking dish.

d. Layer the basil leaves and vegetables on top of the bread slices.

e. In a mixing bowl, whisk together the eggs, milk, pepper, and salt.

f. Pour the egg mixture over the bread and vegetables, making sure to cover everything evenly.

g. Sprinkle cheese on top of the strata.

h. Bake in the preheated oven for 45-50 minutes, or until the top is golden and the strata is set.

i. Remove from the oven and let it cool for a few minutes before serving.

28. Asparagus-Mushroom Frittata

Asparagus-Mushroom Frittata is a delicious and nutritious dish perfect for any time of the day. Loaded with fresh asparagus spears and sautéed mushrooms, this frittata is a flavorful combination of earthy and vibrant flavors. Baked with eggs and cheese, it makes for a satisfying and protein-packed meal.

Preparation Time: 10 minutes

Cook time: 35 minutes

Total: 45 minutes

Serves: 8

Ingredients:

- 1 small onion, diced.
- 8 asparagus spears, trimmed and cut into 1-inch pieces.
- 8 ounces mushrooms, sliced.
- 1 cup shredded cheese (such as cheddar or Gruyere)
- 8 large eggs
- 1/4 cup milk
- 1/2 teaspoon salt
- 1/4 teaspoon black pepper
- 1 tablespoon olive oil

xxxxxxxxxxxxxxxxxxxxxxxxxxxxxxxx

Instructions:

a. Set the oven to 350°F (175°C).

b. In a large bowl, whisk together the eggs, milk, black pepper, and salt.

c. In a large oven-safe skillet over medium heat, warm the olive oil.

d. Cook until the onion is softened, approximately 5 minutes.

e. Add the asparagus and mushrooms to the skillet and cook for another 5 minutes, or until the vegetables are tender.

f. Pour the egg mixture over the vegetables in the skillet.

g. Sprinkle the shredded cheese evenly over the top.

h. Bake for 20-25 minutes, or until the frittata is set and golden brown on top, in the preheated oven.

i. Remove from the oven and let cool for a few minutes before slicing and serving.

29. Spice-Rubbed Chicken Thighs

Spice-Rubbed Chicken Thighs are a flavorful and succulent dish that will delight your taste buds. The chicken thighs are coated in a delicious blend of spices, creating a perfect balance of heat and savory flavors. Whether grilled, roasted, or pan-seared, these chicken thighs are sure to be a crowd-pleasing favorite.

Preparation Time: 10 minutes

Cook time: 35 minutes

Total: 45 minutes

Serves: 6

Ingredients:

- 1 tablespoon garlic powder
- 2 tablespoons olive oil
- 6 chicken thighs
- 1 tablespoon onion powder
- 1 tablespoon dried thyme
- 1 tablespoon salt
- 1 tablespoon black pepper
- 2 tablespoons paprika
- 1 tablespoon ground cumin
- 1 tablespoon ground coriander

xxxxxxxxxxxxxxxxxxxxxxxxxxxxxxxx

Instructions:

a. Set the oven to 425°F (220°C).

b. In a mixing bowl, combine the paprika, garlic powder, onion powder, dried thyme, ground cumin, ground coriander, salt, and black pepper to make the spice rub.

c. Rub the spice mixture evenly over the chicken thighs.

d. Heat the olive oil in a large skillet over medium-high heat.

e. Add the chicken thighs to the skillet and cook for 3-4 minutes on each side until browned.

f. Transfer the chicken thighs to a baking sheet and bake in the preheated oven for 25-30 minutes, or until the internal temperature reaches 165°F (74°C).

g. Remove from the oven and let the chicken thighs rest for a few minutes before serving.

30. Roasted Sweet Potato & Chickpea Pitas

Roasted Sweet Potato & Chickpea Pitas are a delicious and satisfying option for a wholesome meal. The combination of roasted sweet potatoes, crispy chickpeas, and flavorful seasonings creates a delightful filling for warm, soft pitas. This dish offers a balance of textures and flavors, making it a tasty and nutritious choice.

Preparation Time: 10 minutes

Cook time: 35 minutes

Total: 45 minutes

Serves: 6

Ingredients:

- 2 tablespoons olive oil
- 1 teaspoon ground cumin
- 1/2 teaspoon salt
- 1/4 teaspoon black pepper
- 1 cup Greek yogurt
- 1/2 cup chopped fresh cilantro.
- 1/4 cup crumbled feta cheese.
- 2 medium sweet potatoes peeled and cubed.
- 1 can chickpeas drained and rinsed.
- 1 teaspoon ground paprika
- 6 whole wheat pitas
- 1/4 cup diced red onion.

xxxxxxxxxxxxxxxxxxxxxxxxxxxxxxxx

Instructions:

a. Set the oven to 425°F (220°C).

b. In a mixing bowl, combine the sweet potatoes, chickpeas, olive oil, cumin, paprika, salt, and black pepper. Toss until well coated.

c. Spread the mixture onto a baking sheet in a single layer.

d. Roast in the preheated oven for 25-30 minutes, or until the sweet potatoes are tender and slightly caramelized.

e. While the sweet potatoes and chickpeas are roasting, warm the pitas in a toaster or oven.

f. Once the sweet potatoes and chickpeas are done, remove them from the oven and let them cool slightly.

g. To assemble the pitas, spread a spoonful of Greek yogurt onto each pita.

h. Top with the roasted sweet potatoes and chickpeas.

i. Sprinkle with chopped cilantro, diced red onion, and crumbled feta cheese.

j. Fold the pitas in half and serve immediately.

Conclusion

Congratulations on completing This book! You've gained valuable knowledge and practical tools to make clean eating a sustainable part of your lifestyle. Remember, this is not just a temporary diet but a long-term commitment to nourishing your body. By embracing whole, unprocessed foods and practicing mindful eating, you've taken a significant step towards improving your overall health and well-being. As you continue this journey, listen to your body, experiment with new recipes, and find joy in the process of preparing wholesome meals. Make use of the meal planning strategies, label-reading skills, and tips for selecting high-quality ingredients that you've learned from this guide. Remember to stay consistent and be kind to yourself during any slip-ups or challenges along the way.

Wholesome, clean eating is about fueling your body with the nutrients it needs while enjoying the flavors and satisfaction of delicious meals. Embrace this lifestyle and discover the transformative effects it can have on your energy levels, mental clarity, and overall vitality. Cheers to your health and happiness!

Thank you – Thank you – Thank you

I am grateful to you for purchasing and reading my book. It brings me great joy to write, and my motivation stems from my desire to help others. Writing allows me to achieve this goal, and I am grateful for the opportunity to do so.

May I ask what led you to choose this particular book? With so many books and authors exploring similar topics, it means a lot that you chose mine. Your decision is truly appreciated, and I am confident that you will find the book to be immensely beneficial.

I would love to hear your thoughts on the book. As authors, we grow and improve based on the feedback we receive from our readers. Even a small comment or review would be greatly appreciated. Your feedback could even serve as inspiration for other readers. Thank you once again for your support.

Printed in Great Britain
by Amazon

28784931R00044